Thrive

After 70

"The Veteran's Guide to Living Fully and Aging Gracefully"

By

Aaron B. Kershaw

Copyright

This book was a labor of love, with every detail: writing,
cover design, editing, and layout.
by Aaron B. Kershaw.

Language: English

Publication Date: April 2026

Format: Paperback
2nd Edition
ISBN: 979-8-90345-007-7
Cover: Dall-E Photo
Cover Design: Aaron B. Kershaw

Copyright © 2025 Aaron B. Kershaw

All rights reserved. No part of this book may be reproduced, distributed, or transmitted in
any form or by any means, including photocopying, recording, or other electronic or
mechanical methods, without the prior written permission of the publisher, except in the
case of brief quotations embodied in critical reviews and certain other noncommercial
uses permitted by copyright law.

For permission requests, contact the publisher at:

BuildingBlocs Publishing

www.BuildingBlocs.org

akershaw@buildingblocs.org

Thrive After 70: The Veteran's Guide to Living Fully and Aging Gracefully

Published in the United States of America

Table of Contents

Introduction

Part 1: Health and Wellness in the Golden Years

Part 2: Strengthening Relationships and Social Bonds

5. **Friendship for the Long Haul**

    - Reconnecting with old friends and building new friendships.
    - Finding social opportunities in clubs, veterans' groups, and more.
    - Maintaining relationships despite distance or health limitations.

6. **The Technology Bridge**

    - Simplifying technology for staying in touch.
    - Safely navigating the digital world.
    - Apps and tools to make life easier.

Part 3: Rediscovering Purpose and Joy

7. **What₄₅ Next?**

    - Finding purpose through volunteering, mentorship, and hobbies.
    - Discovering new skills and interests.
    - Practical advice on community involvement.

8. **The Power of Storytelling**

    - Capturing and sharing life stories with family and future generations.
    - Journaling prompts and storytelling exercises.
    - Digital and physical methods for documenting history.

9. **Living Fully, Aging Gracefully**

    - Creating a bucket list and embracing new experiences.
    - Exploring travel opportunities and activities on a budget.
    - Staying optimistic and engaged despite challenges.

10. **Resources and Tools for Thriving After 70**

Conclusion: The Next Chapter of Your Journey

    - Reflecting on your next steps.
    - Introduction to Book 2: *"Legacy Secured: Protect Your Finances, Family, and Future."*
    - Encouragement to build your legacy and live fully every day.

A Letter from Uncle Aaron

Hey there, my fellow road warriors,

I know you've got a lot of stories. How do I know? Because you've lived through some of the biggest chapters in history. You were young when The Beatles were on the radio and when we were watching Armstrong Walk on the moon. You've seen wars start and end, watched technology evolve from rotary phones to FaceTime, and witnessed your grandkids growing up with apps you still don't fully trust. Let me tell you, you've been through the ringer and back, and here you are, still standing.

This book isn't about telling you what you've already lived. This is about the next chapter, the one where *you* are in charge. The one where you stop living in survival mode and start thriving. Sure, there are some aches and pains, some silver hairs (or none at all), but you've still got a whole lot of life left to live. And it's my job as your "younger" Uncle Aaron (all 54 years of me) to help you do that with purpose, joy, and maybe a few belly laughs along the way.

I'm not here to sugarcoat anything. Life after 70 comes with its challenges. Loneliness, health scares, figuring out how to make Social Security stretch further than you thought possible, it's real, and it's tough. But you've fought tougher battles than this. You've earned the right to live well, laugh often, and enjoy the time you have without constantly worrying about what's next.

What This Book Is About

This book is my way of sitting down with you over a cup of coffee (or a cold beer if it's after noon) and talking through the things that really matter staying healthy, keeping meaningful relationships alive, and finding purpose again in a world that's changed a lot since the Vietnam days.

We'll cover the practical stuff, like how to keep your body moving, eat better without turning into a rabbit, and use your phone for more than just getting calls from telemarketers. But we'll also dive into the deeper stuff: how to find joy again, how to reconnect with family, and how to leave a legacy that makes you proud.

Why I Wrote This Book

Because the truth is, no one really prepares us for what comes after 70. It's not just about staying alive; it's about living in a way that makes you feel alive. And trust me, it's never too late. Whether you're feeling stuck, lonely, or just unsure about how to navigate this next phase, I promise this book will give you the tools and mindset to take control and start thriving.

I've seen firsthand how veterans like you, tough as nails, but with a lifetime of wisdom, can use what you've learned to tackle anything life throws your way. I've also seen how easy it is to get stuck in your ways, to let time pass you by because you're too busy looking back. My job? To remind you that you've got a whole lot of looking forward left to do.

How This Book Works

Each chapter is designed to be a conversation, just you and me, talking it out. You'll find practical advice, a touch of humor (because if we can't laugh at ourselves, who will?), and easy-to-follow action steps. This isn't about reinventing yourself, it's about rediscovering what makes you *you* and using that to build a life you're excited to wake up to every day.

- **Part 1:** We'll tackle health and wellness. I'll show you how to keep moving, eat well, and stay sharp without feeling like you're prepping for boot camp again.

- **Part 2:** We'll focus on relationships, because even the strongest among us need connection. From family to friends, we'll rebuild those bonds that matter most.

- **Part 3:** Finally, we'll dive into purpose and joy. Whether it's picking up a new hobby, giving back to your community, or finally writing that memoir, we'll make sure you have a reason to smile every day.

What I Hope You'll Take Away

By the end of this book, I hope you'll feel more confident, more connected, and more in control of your life. I want you to see aging not as the end of the road, but as the beginning of a whole new adventure. You've got wisdom, grit, and a lifetime of experience, and now, it's time to put that to use in a way that makes everyday count.

So, let's get to it. Grab a pen, take some notes, and let's make this next chapter your best yet.

With respect, humor, and a lot of heart,
Uncle Aaron

Chapter 1:

Your Body's Second Act

"Aging Ain't for the Weak, but You're Stronger Than You Think"

Let's be real for a minute: Aging isn't for the faint of heart. Your body has been your ride or die for decades, carrying you through battles, raising families, building careers, and all the curveballs life has thrown at you. But now, it might feel like it's starting to fight back, knees that creak, backs that ache, and energy that doesn't quite keep up with your ambitions. It's easy to think, "I guess this is just how it is now." But here's the thing: it doesn't have to be.

This chapter isn't about pretending you can turn back the clock. It's about recognizing that, even now, your body has the potential for strength, resilience, and growth. Think of this as your second act, the part of your story where you redefine what thriving looks like, not by ignoring the changes of aging, but by understanding and adapting to them.

Your body has been through a lot, and it deserves care, respect, and some solid maintenance. Let's talk about how to give it exactly that.

What's Happening Under the Hood?

Before we dive into the "how," let's look at the "why." What's actually going on with your body as you age? A lot of the challenges you're experiencing, stiffness, slower recovery, or chronic pain, are normal, but they don't have to define you. Understanding these changes is the first step to taking control.

1. Muscle Loss: The Reality of Sarcopenia

By your 70s, you've likely lost 25–30% of the muscle mass you had in your younger years. This process, called **sarcopenia**, starts around age 30 and accelerates after 60. Why? Your body's ability to synthesize protein slows down, and if you're not actively using your muscles, your body figures, "Hey, guess we don't need this anymore."

But here's the good news: **Muscle loss isn't a one-way street.** Even people in their 80s can rebuild muscle mass with regular resistance training. The key is consistency. You don't need to lift heavy weights; even simple bodyweight exercises like chair squats or wall push-ups can make a huge difference.

2. Joint Stiffness: The Price of Mileage

Your joints are like the hinges on a well-loved door. Over decades of movement, wear and tear are inevitable. Cartilage things, and your body produces less synovial fluid, the lubricant that keeps things moving smoothly.

That's why movement is essential. Harvard Medical School found that **regular low-impact exercise** like walking, swimming, or tai chi reduces stiffness and **stimulates joint fluid production**. Motion, quite literally, is lotion.

3. Bone Density: Building a Stronger Foundation

After 30, bones begin to lose density, a process that speeds up after 50, especially in women. Conditions like **osteopenia** or **osteoporosis** increase fracture risk. But your bones are living tissue; they respond to stress by growing stronger.

Weight-bearing exercises (light resistance training, uphill walking) combined with a **calcium- and vitamin D-rich diet** (leafy greens, dairy, salmon) can help reinforce bone strength.

Managing Pain Without Letting It Control You

Living with chronic pain? You're not alone. Whether arthritis, old injuries, or accumulated wear and tear, pain can feel like a constant companion. But it doesn't have to control you.

1. Stretching for Relief

Stretching improves blood flow, reduces tension, and eases joint pain. Start small:

- **Neck rolls** for tension
- **Forward bends** for your back
- **Seated twists** for spinal mobility

Just **five minutes a day** can make a big difference.

2. Alternatives to Pain Meds

OTC painkillers are useful, but explore non-pharmaceutical options:

- **Tai Chi & Yoga**: Improve flexibility and reduce pain
- **Aqua Therapy**: Low-impact strength-building in water
- **Acupuncture**: NIH studies show it can reduce chronic pain by up to 50%

3. The Role of Mindfulness

Pain isn't just physical. **Mindfulness and meditation** can train you to observe pain without being consumed by it. Mindfulness-Based Stress Reduction (MBSR) programs have been shown to lower pain intensity and improve quality of life.

Movement: The Fountain of Youth

Movement isn't about vanity, it's about function. **Regular movement improves mood, balance, heart health, and joint function.**

A Simple Movement Routine for Every Level

Beginner (Seated):

- Toe Taps (x10)
- Seated Marches (x15)

Intermediate:

- Chair Squats (x10–12)
- Wall Push-Ups (x8–10)

Advanced:

- Step-Ups (x10)
- Light Dumbbell Lifts (e.g., curls, presses)

Motivation: The Key to Consistency

It's normal to have off days. The trick? Anchor yourself in your *why*.

Tips for Staying Motivated

- **Track Progress:** Journal what you did, how you felt, what you're proud of.
- **Set Small Goals:** Walk 5 minutes, do 10 squats, celebrate wins.
- **Find Your Why:** Grandkids, independence, travel, keep that purpose in sight.

Action Step: Make a Commitment

Grab a piece of paper and write down:

1. One movement goal for this week (e.g., "I'll Walk 10 minutes a day")

2. How you'll track your progress

3. One thing your body has done for you that you're grateful for

Conclusion: Your Second Act Starts Now

This isn't about chasing your 20s. It's about honoring your present body and investing in your future.

"You've carried the weight of the world. Now let's make sure your body carries you through the best years still ahead."

Chapter 2:

Fueling the Machine

"Eating for Strength, Energy, and the Life You Want to Live"

Let me guess. You've heard it all before, "Eat more vegetables. Stay hydrated. Cut back on the sweets." Sound familiar? Probably because your doctor has been saying the same thing for years. But here's the thing: I know you're not looking for another lecture. What you want is real, practical advice that works for *your* life. Not one-size-fits-all. Not "diet trends." Just straight talk about how to eat in a way that gives you energy, strength, and maybe even a little joy.

This isn't about deprivation or becoming a kale-worshipping fitness guru. It's about learning how to fuel your body in a way that keeps you thriving. Because here's the truth: what you eat impacts *everything*, your energy, your mood, your sleep, your ability to get up in the morning without feeling like you've been hit by a truck. Let's make sure you're giving your body what it needs to take on whatever the day throws at you.

Your Nutrition Game Plan: Veteran Edition

Let's take a no-BS approach. Your body has been through wars, literally. Whether it was chow hall meals, MREs, or the miracle of a hot home-cooked dinner, you've probably eaten it all. But just like your service gear needed maintenance and care, your body does, too. And after 70, the type of fuel you put in matters more than ever. Here's why:

Why Nutrition Changes After 70

1. **Metabolism Hits the Brakes**
   Think of your metabolism as a campfire. When you were young, it burned hot and fast, meaning you could eat almost anything and still feel ready to charge ahead. Now, that fire has slowed, and your body doesn't burn calories the way it used to. Overeating, even on healthy foods, can lead to weight gain, while undereating can leave you feeling drained.

Translation: It's time to get strategic. Smaller portions, more nutrient-dense foods, and spreading your meals throughout the day will keep your energy steady.

2. **Your Body Needs More, Not Less**
   Here's the kicker: while you need fewer calories, you actually need **more nutrients**. Your body gets worse at absorbing vitamins and minerals like calcium, Vitamin D, and B12. That means a diet filled with empty calories (looking at you, potato chips) leaves you running on fumes.

3. **Food Is Medicine**
   Chronic conditions like high blood pressure, arthritis, or diabetes can often be improved, or even prevented, with the right diet. For example, foods high in Omega-3s (like salmon or walnuts) can reduce inflammation, while leafy greens support heart health.

The Veteran's Nutrition Plan: Mission-Focused Eating

Here's the plan: no fads, no complicated rules, just practical, easy-to-follow advice. Let's focus on what *works*.

1. Build Your Plate Like You Built a Unit

In the military, every role mattered, whether it was logistics, front-line action, or support. Your meals should work the same way, with every food playing a role:

- **The Front Line (Protein):** This is your muscle builder. Protein supports strength, healing, and energy. Think grilled chicken, eggs, lean beef, beans, or Greek yogurt. You need about 70–90 grams of protein daily.

- **The Backup (Veggies and Fruits):** These are your reinforcements, packed with vitamins, fiber, and antioxidants. Aim for half your plate to be veggies or fruits. The more colorful, the better, think spinach, carrots, berries, and oranges.

- **The Fuel (Whole Grains):** These give you the energy to keep going. Choose whole grains like brown rice, quinoa, or whole-grain bread. They digest slowly, keeping you fuller longer.

2. Shift from "Big Meals" to "Strategic Snacking"

Back in the day, you might've been fine with three big meals. But now, your body likes things in smaller doses. Eating every 3–4 hours keeps your blood sugar steady and your energy up.

Example Meal Plan:

- **Breakfast:** Scrambled eggs with spinach and whole-grain toast.

- **Snack:** A handful of almonds and an apple.

- **Lunch:** Turkey sandwich with a side of mixed greens and olive oil dressing.

- **Snack:** Greek yogurt with fresh berries.

- **Dinner:** Baked salmon with roasted sweet potatoes and steamed broccoli.

3. The $50 Weekly Meal Strategy

Here's where the practical side kicks in. You don't need to spend a fortune or cook gourmet meals to eat well. Here's a simple $50 grocery list that covers all the bases:

- **Proteins:** Eggs, canned tuna, chicken breasts, lentils.

- **Veggies:** Frozen broccoli, carrots, spinach.

- **Fruits:** Bananas, apples, a bag of frozen berries.

- **Whole Grains:** Oatmeal, brown rice, whole-grain bread.

- **Extras:** Olive oil, Greek yogurt, peanut butter.

Hydration: The Forgotten Secret Weapon

Let's talk water. Dehydration isn't just about being thirsty, it affects your energy, digestion, and even your memory. After 70, your body's thirst signals become weaker, meaning you might not realize you're dehydrated until it's already affecting you.

The Hydration Checklist:

1. **Aim for 8–10 cups daily.** Keep a water bottle nearby as a visual reminder.

2. **Hydrating Foods:** Eat water-rich foods like watermelon, cucumbers, and oranges.

3. **Herbal Teas:** If plain water bores you, try herbal teas (no caffeine!) to mix things up.

Bonus Tip: If you're waking up with muscle cramps at night, dehydration could be the culprit. Drinking a glass of water before bed might just save you from those 3 a.m. charley horses.

Let's Bust Some Nutrition Myths

You've probably heard a lot of conflicting advice over the years. Let's separate fact from fiction:

Myth #1: "Fat Is Bad for You"
Not true. Healthy fats (like avocados, olive oil, and nuts) are essential for brain health and energy. The bad guys are trans fats and too much saturated fat.

Myth #2: "Carbs Make You Gain Weight"
Carbs aren't the enemy; it's the type of carbs that matter. Skip the white bread and pastries and opt for whole grains like oatmeal or quinoa.

Myth #3: "You Don't Need Supplements"
While food is the best source of nutrients, some supplements (like Vitamin D or B12) can help fill in the gaps. Talk to your doctor about what's right for you.

Why Weight Management Looks Different After 70

Weight isn't just about looks; it's about staying mobile and reducing strain on your joints. But here's the thing: this isn't the time for extreme diets or drastic changes. Instead, focus on balance and sustainability.

The 3 Keys to Managing Weight:

1. **Focus on Quality, Not Calories:** A nutrient-dense meal will keep you full longer than a calorie-heavy one.

2. **Stay Active:** Even a short daily walk burns calories and improves metabolism.

3. **Be Patient:** Progress takes time, and that's okay.

Action Steps for the Week

Let's make this actionable. Here's what I want you to do this week:

1. **Write a Grocery List:** Plan 3 days of meals using the $50 strategy.

2. **Track Your Water:** Note how many cups of water you're drinking each day.

3. **Add One New Food:** Try something you haven't had in a while, maybe salmon, lentils, or a colorful veggie.

Conclusion: Eating for Strength and Longevity

Fueling your body doesn't have to be complicated, expensive, or boring. It's about small, intentional choices that add up overtime. The better you eat, the better you'll feel, and that means more energy, more strength, and more good days ahead.

"Your body has carried you through a lot. Feed it well, and it'll carry you through the best that's yet to come."

Chapter 3:

Mental Wellness Matters

"Your Mind Is Your Strongest Weapon, Keep It Sharp"

You've seen a lot in your lifetime, some of it joyful, some of it hard, and some of it downright impossible to forget. Over the years, your mind has carried the weight of memories, lessons, and a million small decisions. But just like your body, your mind needs care and attention to stay sharp and resilient.

If you've been feeling stressed, lonely, or just plain "off," you're not alone. Life after 70 comes with its own set of challenges. Maybe your social circle has gotten smaller, or the things that used to bring you joy don't hit the same anymore. Maybe you've caught yourself thinking, *"Why do I feel this way? I've been through worse."* But here's the thing: your mental health deserves just as much attention as your physical health.

This chapter is about giving your mind the tools it needs to not just survive but thrive. We're going to tackle stress, loneliness, and mental sharpness head-on, with practical tips you can start using today.

Why Mental Wellness Matters More Than Ever

Let's start with the big picture. Why does mental wellness become even more important as we age? Because your mental health affects everything, from how you process physical pain to how you connect with others and enjoy your day-to-day life.

1. *The Mind-Body Connection*

    Stress and negative emotions don't just stay in your head; they show up in your body. Chronic stress can cause headaches, high blood pressure, and even weaken your immune system. But the flip side is also true: positive mental health can reduce pain, improve sleep, and boost your energy levels.

2. *Social Circles Change Over Time*

    By this stage of life, your social world might look a lot different than it did 20 or 30 years ago. Friends move away, families get busier, and sometimes we lose people we love. These changes can lead to feelings of isolation or loneliness, which are more common than you think.

3. *Staying Sharp*

    Your brain is like a muscle, the more you use it, the stronger it stays. Mental sharpness is critical for independence and quality of life, and there are ways to actively protect and improve your cognitive health.

Addressing Stress

Let's talk about stress. Whether it's worrying about money, health, or simply the unpredictability of life, stress doesn't magically disappear as we age. But the way you handle it can make all the difference.

1. What Stress Does to Your Body

When you're stressed, your body releases **cortisol**, a hormone designed to help you handle short-term threats. But when stress becomes chronic, that cortisol doesn't shut off, leading to:

- Increased blood pressure.

- Trouble sleeping.

- Reduced immune function.

Think of it like leaving a car engine running all night, it's going to burn out faster than if it were turned off.

2. Simple Tools to Manage Stress

Here's the good news: you don't need to eliminate stress (that's impossible), but you can learn to manage it.

Breathe Like You Mean It

When you're stressed, your breathing becomes shallow, which sends signals to your brain that something's wrong. A simple breathing exercise can help reset your system:

- Breathe in deeply for a count of four.

- Hold your breath for four counts.

- Exhale slowly for a count of six. Repeat this three times, and you'll feel your heart rate slow.

The "10-Minute Rule"

Stress loves to pile on when you're overwhelmed. The solution? Break tasks into small, 10-minute chunks. Focus on what you can do right now, not everything you need to do eventually.

Physical Release

Stress doesn't just live in your head; it lives in your body. A quick walk, some light stretching, or even clenching and releasing your fists can help release that pent-up tension.

Combating Loneliness

Loneliness isn't just an emotional issue; it's a health risk. Studies have shown that prolonged loneliness can increase your risk of heart disease, depression, and even dementia. But here's the thing: you don't need a massive social circle to feel connected. You just need a few meaningful interactions.

1. The Power of Connection

Humans are wired for connection. Whether it's sharing a meal with family, chatting with an old friend, or even saying hello to your neighbor, these small moments of connection matter.

- **Reach Out**

    If you've lost touch with someone, take the first step. Send a text, write a letter, or make a quick call. Most people are happy to reconnect; they're just waiting for someone to make the first move.

- **Volunteer**

    Helping others is one of the quickest ways to combat loneliness. Whether it's mentoring younger veterans, working at a food bank, or even walking dogs at a local shelter, volunteering gives you a sense of purpose and connection.

2. Modern Tools for Staying Social

Technology can be a lifeline for staying connected. If you're not already using tools like Zoom, FaceTime, or even Facebook, consider giving them a try. They're simpler than you think, and they can help you feel closer to loved ones, even if they're far away.

Staying Mentally Sharp

You might've heard the phrase, *"Use it or lose it."* That's because your brain needs stimulation to stay sharp. The good news? Keeping your mind active can be fun.

1. Brain-Boosting Activities

- **Learn Something New**
  Whether it's picking up a new hobby, learning a language, or even trying out a new recipe, challenging your brain helps build new neural connections.

- **Play Games**
  Crosswords, Sudoku, chess, or even puzzles are more than just fun, they're workouts for your brain.

- **Read and Write**
  Reading keeps your brain engaged, while writing, whether it's journaling, storytelling, or even jotting down grocery lists, improves memory and focus.

2. Feed Your Brain

What you eat matters for your mental health. Foods like salmon, walnuts, blueberries, and dark chocolate are known to boost brain health. Think of them as fuel for your mental engine.

Mindfulness and Gratitude

If the idea of meditation or mindfulness makes you roll your eyes, hear me out. Mindfulness isn't about sitting cross-legged and chanting, it's about learning to be present in the moment.

1. What Is Mindfulness?

Mindfulness is the practice of focusing your attention on the present. Instead of worrying about tomorrow or regretting yesterday, it's about noticing what's happening right now.

2. A Simple Gratitude Practice

Gratitude is one of the most powerful tools for mental wellness. Here's an exercise to try:

- Each morning, write down three things you're grateful for. They can be as simple as, *"The coffee tastes good today."*

- Reflect on those things throughout the day. Gratitude shifts your focus from what's wrong to what's right.

3. Beginner's Meditation

If you're new to meditation, start with just two minutes:

1. Sit comfortably and close your eyes.

2. Focus on your breath. Notice the sensation of air entering and leaving your nose.

3. When your mind wanders (and it will), gently bring it back to your breath.

Recognizing Depression

Sometimes, feeling "off" goes beyond stress or loneliness. Depression is a serious issue, and it's more common in older adults than many realize. The good news? It's treatable.

1. Signs of Depression

- Persistent sadness or irritability.
- Loss of interest in things you used to enjoy.
- Changes in appetite or sleep.
- Feeling hopeless or worthless.

2. When to Seek Help

If these feelings last for more than two weeks, it's time to talk to someone. Reach out to your doctor, a counselor, or a trusted friend. Asking for help isn't a sign of weakness, it's a sign of strength.

Action Steps for the Week

Here's your mental wellness homework:

1. **Reconnect**: Call or message one person you haven't spoken to in a while.

2. **Try Mindfulness**: Spend two minutes each day focusing on your breath.

3. **Write It Down**: Start a gratitude journal and jot down three things you're thankful for each morning.

Conclusion: Strengthening Your Mind

Your mind is one of the greatest tools you have. With a little care, attention, and practice, you can keep it sharp, resilient, and ready for whatever comes next. Mental wellness isn't about perfection, it's about showing up for yourself every day.

"You've faced battles no one else can imagine. This is just another one, and I know you've got the strength to win it."

Part 2:

Strengthening Relationships & Social Bonds

Thrive After 70: "The Veteran's Guide to Living Fully and Aging Gracefully"

Chapter Four

Staying Connected to Loved Ones

"Family Isn't Perfect, but It's Always Worth It"

Family, what a beautifully complicated thing. It can be a source of immense joy and comfort, or it can feel like walking through a minefield. Sometimes, it's both at the same time. But no matter what your family looks like, whether it's big, small, close-knit, or spread out, it's the relationships we have with our loved ones that shape the legacy we leave behind.

As you get older, those relationships can shift. Your kids may have kids of their own now. Conversations might not flow as easily as they once did. Maybe you've caught yourself thinking, *"Why don't I hear from them more often?"* or *"Do they even understand what I've been through?"* These gaps can feel wide, but they're not unbridgeable.

This chapter is about closing those gaps. It's about practical ways to strengthen your relationships with your children, grandchildren, and the people who matter most. Family may not always be easy, but it's always worth it.

The Changing Dynamics of Family

Let's start with a hard truth: family relationships change. It's natural. The kids you once carried on your shoulders are now carrying the weight of their own lives, careers, mortgages, raising their kids, and keeping up with the chaos of modern life. They love you, but their schedules don't always leave much room for phone calls or visits.

And then there's the generation gap. You grew up in a world without smartphones, social media, or TikTok dances (thank goodness, right?). Your kids and grandkids live in a different reality, one that's often more fast-paced, more digital, and, let's face it, harder to understand. It's easy to feel like you're speaking different languages.

But here's the good news: love doesn't need translation. It just needs effort, patience, and a willingness to meet each other halfway.

Strengthening Relationships with Children and Grandchildren

1. Understanding Their World

It's easy to look at the younger generation and think, *"They have no idea how good they've got it."* And maybe that's true. But here's the flip side: the challenges they face, like constant pressure from social media or juggling work and family, are real, even if they look different from what you experienced.

What You Can Do:
Start with curiosity, not judgment. Ask questions about their world. What's a typical day like for them? What are they excited about? What's been stressing them out? Listening without jumping in to "fix" things shows you care about their experiences.

2. Showing Up (Even From Afar)

You don't need grand gestures to show your family you're there for them. Consistency matters more than anything. A quick text, a phone call, or even a postcard lets them know you're thinking of them.

Pro Tip: Set reminders. If you're worried about forgetting birthdays, anniversaries, or just checking in, set a calendar reminder. It's a small step that makes a big difference.

3. Making Time for One-on-One Moments

Group gatherings are great, but there's something special about one-on-one time. Whether it's grabbing coffee with your adult child or having a video call with a grandkid, those personal connections strengthen bonds.

What You Can Say: "I'd love to spend some time with you one-on-one. Let me know what works for you."

Bridging the Generational Gap

Let's face it: kids these days (even adult ones) have a totally different set of tools and experiences than you did. But instead of letting that difference feel like a wall, let's turn it into a bridge.

1. Conversation Starters That Work

It's easy to feel like you don't have much to talk about, especially with younger family members. But the truth is, they're often just waiting for you to ask.

Here are some go-to conversation starters:

For Your Kids:

- "What's been the most rewarding part of being a parent? What's been the hardest?"
- "Tell me about your job, what's your favorite part of what you do?"

For Your Grandkids:

- "What's your favorite subject in school right now?"
- "What's something cool you learned recently?"
- "Can you teach me something about your favorite game/app/TV show?"

2. Embracing Their Interests (Even If You Don't Get It)

Here's the thing about kids and grandkids: they love it when you take an interest in what they're passionate about. Maybe it's a sport, a video game, or even a TikTok trend. You don't have to understand it fully, you just have to care.

Example: Ask your grandkids to show you how to play their favorite video game or explain the latest meme. It's not about the activity itself; it's about showing you value their world.

The Importance of Family Traditions and Regular Connections

Family traditions are more than just routines, they're anchors. They give your family a sense of continuity, belonging, and identity. And they're something you, as the elder of the family, can pass down.

1. Reviving Old Traditions

Think back to the traditions that meant something to you growing up. Sunday dinners, holiday rituals, or even small things like game nights or movie marathons. What can you bring back?

What You Can Do: Suggest reviving an old tradition with a modern twist. For example, if you used to have family BBQs, make it a potluck where everyone brings a dish.

2. Creating New Traditions

Your family is constantly growing and evolving, which means it's the perfect time to start something new. Maybe it's an annual camping trip, a monthly Zoom call, or a family recipe book where everyone contributes.

> **Pro Tip:** Make it simple. Traditions don't have to be elaborate; they just need to be consistent.

3. Making Connections a Habit

> Connection isn't just about the big moments; it's about the everyday ones. A quick phone call, a shared meal, or even a weekly check-in can go a long way in keeping family bonds strong.

What to Do When Relationships Feel Strained

Not all family relationships are smooth sailing. Sometimes, misunderstandings, hurt feelings, or long periods of silence can create distance. The good news? It's never too late to try to mend those bonds.

1. Start with Grace

> If there's tension, approach the situation with grace. Instead of rehashing old arguments, focus on what you can do moving forward.
>
> **What You Can Say:** "I know we haven't always seen eye to eye, but I'd really like for us to move forward. How can we do that?"

2. Accept What You Can't Change

> Sometimes, despite your best efforts, not every relationship will look the way you hoped. And that's okay. Focus on the connections that bring you joy and peace, and let go of the ones that drain you.

Action Steps for the Week

Here's your family connection mission:

1. **Make a Call:** Reach out to one family member this week, just to check in and say hi.

2. **Start a Tradition:** Think of one simple way to connect regularly with your family (a weekly Zoom call, Sunday dinners, etc.).

3. **Ask a Question:** Use one of the conversation starters above to spark a meaningful chat.

Conclusion: Love Is in the Effort

Staying connected with your family isn't about being perfect; it's about showing up. It's about making the effort to bridge gaps, spark conversations, and create moments of connection that matter. You've built a lifetime of wisdom, love, and stories, don't keep them to yourself. Share them with the people who matter most.

"Family isn't about being the same, it's about loving through the differences."

Chapter Five

Friendship for the Long Haul

"Because the Right Friends Make Every Year Better"

Let's face it, friends make life richer. They're the people who've shared laughs, tears, and maybe a few beers with you over the years. But as we get older, it's easy for friendships to slip through the cracks. Life gets busy, people move, and before you know it, months or years can pass without a word.

But here's the thing: it's never too late to reconnect, and it's never too late to build new friendships, either. The relationships you have, whether they're decades old or brand new, are some of the most powerful tools you have for staying happy, healthy, and grounded. Studies have shown that maintaining strong social ties can boost your immune system, reduce stress, and even help you live longer.

In this chapter, we're going to talk about how to reconnect with old friends, build new relationships, and keep those bonds strong, no matter where life takes you. Because if there's one thing I know for sure, it's this: friendship is worth the effort.

Why Friendships Matter More Than Ever

As we age, our priorities shift. Careers slow down, kids move out, and for some of us, we lose loved ones who were pillars of our social circles. That's why investing in friendships becomes so important.

Here's why good friends are worth their weight in gold:

1. **They Keep You Mentally Sharp:** Conversations, shared activities, and even friendly debates stimulate your brain in ways that solitary activities can't.

2. **They Support Your Health:** Studies from the Mayo Clinic show that strong social connections can reduce the risk of depression, improve cardiovascular health, and increase life expectancy.

3. **They Bring Joy:** Simply put, friends make life more fun. They're the people who remind you to laugh, even when things get tough.

If you've been feeling lonely or disconnected, you're not alone. The good news? There are countless ways to rebuild those connections and strengthen the ones you already have.

Reconnecting with Old Friends

Let's start with the easy wins. You don't have to reinvent the wheel when it comes to friendship. Sometimes, the best relationships are the ones you already have, waiting to be rekindled.

1. Taking the First Step

Think about the people who've meant the most to you over the years. Maybe it's a buddy from your military days, an old coworker, or even a childhood friend you haven't seen in decades. Now ask yourself: Why not reach out?

- **What to Say:** "Hey [Name], I was thinking about you the other day and realized it's been way too long since we caught up. How have you been?"

- **Pro Tip:** If you're nervous about starting the conversation, keep it light. Share a funny memory, mention something that reminded you of them, or ask about something they were passionate about.

2. Embracing the Awkward

Reconnecting can feel a little awkward at first, especially if it's been a long time. But here's the thing: most people are thrilled to hear from someone who genuinely cares about them. Don't let fear hold you back.

Building New Friendships

Sometimes, life takes us in directions where our old friends aren't as close as they used to be, physically or emotionally. That's where making new friends comes in. And yes, it's possible to make new friends at any age.

1. Finding Your People

The key to building new friendships is putting yourself in places where connections can happen. Here are a few great places to start:

- **Local Clubs:** Whether it's a book club, a gardening group, or a walking club, shared interests make it easier to connect.

- **Veterans' Groups:** Organizations like the VFW or American Legion are great places to meet people who've walked a similar path.

- **Volunteer Opportunities:** Helping others is a powerful way to meet like-minded people while making a difference in your community.

- **Senior Centers or Community Programs:** Many towns offer classes, events, or social groups designed to bring people together.

2. Starting Small

Making new friends doesn't mean you have to dive into deep conversations right away. Start with small, casual interactions, a smile, a greeting, or a quick chat about the weather. Those small moments can lay the foundation for deeper connections.

Maintaining Relationships Despite Distance or Health Challenges

Life has a way of throwing curveballs, whether it's a friend moving across the country or health issues that make it harder to get out and about. But that doesn't mean you have to let those friendships fade.

1. Staying Connected from Afar

Thanks to technology, it's easier than ever to stay in touch with friends, no matter where they are.

- **Video Calls:** Apps like Zoom or FaceTime let you see each other, even if you're miles apart.

- **Texting and Email:** A quick message to say, "I'm thinking of you," can go a long way.

- **Snail Mail:** Never underestimate the power of a handwritten letter or postcard. It's personal, thoughtful, and unexpected in the best way.

2. Adapting to Health Limitations

If getting out of the house isn't as easy as it used to be, there are still ways to maintain your friendships:

- **Host at Home:** If mobility is an issue, invite friends over for coffee, tea, or a game night.

- **Virtual Hangouts:** Suggest watching a movie "together" over a video call or starting a virtual book club.

- **Short Outings:** Even a brief walk in the park or a trip to a local café can be a meaningful way to spend time with a friend.

Tips for Nurturing Friendships

Friendships don't maintain themselves, they need attention and care, just like any relationship. Here are a few simple ways to keep your connections strong:

1. Be the One Who Reaches Out

Don't wait for your friends to make the first move. Whether it's a text, a call, or a quick note, being proactive shows, you care.

2. Celebrate the Small Stuff

You don't need a big occasion to connect. Celebrate the little things, a sunny day, a new book recommendation, or even a shared memory that makes you laugh.

3. Be Present

When you're with your friends, give them your full attention. Put down the phone, listen actively, and show that you value the time you're spending together.

Friendship Success Stories

Let me tell you about Bob and Mike, two veterans who reconnected after 30 years. Bob stumbled across an old photo of the two of them during their service and decided to track Mike down through a mutual acquaintance. That one phone call turned into regular coffee meetups, and now they're closer than ever.

Friendship doesn't have an expiration date. Whether it's reconnecting with an old buddy or making a new friend, it's never too late to strengthen the relationships that matter.

Action Steps for the Week

Here's your friendship mission:

1. **Reach Out:** Contact one old friend you haven't spoken to in a while.

2. **Explore Opportunities:** Look up a local club, class, or volunteer opportunity and commit to checking it out.

3. **Strengthen What You Have:** Send a quick message or note to a current friend, just to let them know you're thinking of them.

Conclusion: Friendship Is a Choice

Friendships don't just happen, they're built, maintained, and sometimes rebuilt. The good news? Every step you take to strengthen your friendships, old or new, pays off in ways you can't always measure. They'll make you laugh, lift you up, and remind you that you're never alone.

"The best ships are friendships, because they carry you through life's greatest journeys."

Chapter 6:

The Technology Bridge

"Building Connections One Tap at a Time"

If there's one thing that's changed the world more than anything else in the past few decades, it's technology. Phones have gone from being stuck to the wall to fitting in your pocket, and now, they do everything from sending messages to ordering groceries. I know what you're thinking: *"I've lived this long without knowing how to 'FaceTime,' so why start now?"* But here's the thing: technology isn't just for the kids. It's for anyone who wants to stay connected, simplify their life, and maybe even have a little fun along the way.

This chapter is your roadmap to navigating the digital world. I'll show you how to use technology to stay in touch with family and friends, avoid scams, and even make your life a little easier. Don't worry, you don't need to be a tech wizard. All you need is an open mind and a willingness to try. Let's build this bridge together.

Why Technology Matters for Connection

Before we get into the how, let's talk about the why. Why should you bother with texting, Zoom calls, or email when you've made it this far without them? The answer is simple: because the people you care about are using them.

Technology has become the way we connect with family, friends, and the world around us. It's how your grandkids share their school pictures, how your kids invite you to family events, and how friends stay in touch across the miles. If you're not using it, you're missing out on opportunities to stay close, even when you're far apart.

Simplifying Technology for Staying in Touch

Let's start with the basics: how to use the tools that make staying connected easy.

1. Texting: The Modern-Day Postcard

Texting is one of the simplest ways to communicate. It's quick, easy, and perfect for sending short messages like "Thinking of you" or "How are you?" You don't need to write a novel, just a sentence or two will do.

How to Text:

1. Open the "Messages" app on your phone.

2. Tap the pencil or "+" icon to start a new message.

3. Type the recipient's name or phone number, write your message, and hit send.

Pro Tip: If typing feels tricky, try using the microphone icon on your keyboard to dictate your message. Speak clearly, and your phone will do the typing for you.

2. Zoom and Video Calls: Face-to-Face, Anywhere

Zoom, FaceTime, and other video call apps let you see and talk to loved ones in real time. Imagine sitting at your kitchen table and "visiting" with your grandkids who live across the country, it's the next best thing to being there in person.

Getting Started with Zoom:

1. Download the Zoom app from your phone or tablet's app store.

2. Create a free account using your email address.

3. When someone invites you to a Zoom call, click the link they send you, and you'll join the call.

Pro Tip: Schedule regular video calls with family or friends. Whether it's a weekly chat or a monthly check-in, having it on the calendar makes it easier to stay connected.

3. Email: Your Digital Mailbox

Email might not be as trendy as texting or video calls, but it's still one of the best ways to share updates, send photos, or stay in touch with people who prefer written communication.

How to Use Email:

1. Open your email app (like Gmail or Yahoo Mail).

2. Tap "Compose" or the pencil icon to start a new message.

3. Enter the recipient's email address, type your message, and hit send.

Pro Tip: Create an email folder for family updates. That way, you can easily find messages about birthdays, events, or shared photos without scrolling endlessly.

Safely Navigating the Digital World

The internet is full of opportunities, but it also has its share of pitfalls. Scams, phishing emails, and fraudsters are always on the lookout for unsuspecting targets. The good news? A little caution goes a long way.

1. Spotting Scams and Phishing Emails

Scammers often pose as legitimate companies or even family members to trick you into giving away personal information. Here's how to stay safe:

Red Flags of a Scam:

- The message asks for your personal information, like your Social Security number or bank account details.
- The sender's email address doesn't match the company name (e.g., a Netflix email from "support@random123.com").
- The message creates urgency, saying things like "Act now to avoid penalties!"

What to Do:

- Don't click on any links or download attachments.
- Verify the message by contacting the company directly using their official website or phone number.
- Delete the email if it seems suspicious.

2. Password Safety

Think of your passwords as the keys to your digital house. Make them strong, and don't use the same one for everything.

Tips for Strong Passwords:

- Use at least 12 characters, including letters, numbers, and symbols.
- Avoid using personal information like your name or birthday.

- Consider using a password manager app to store and create secure passwords.

Apps and Tools That Make Life Easier

Technology isn't just for staying connected, it can also simplify your daily life. Here are a few apps and tools worth exploring:

1. Communication Tools

- **WhatsApp:** A free messaging app that lets you text, call, and send photos to anyone in the world.

- **Marco Polo:** A video messaging app that lets you send "video postcards" to friends and family.

2. Health and Wellness Apps

- **Pill Reminder - Meds Alarm:** Helps you track and remember to take your medications.

- **MyFitnessPal:** A simple app for tracking your meals and physical activity.

3. Convenience Apps

- **Instacart:** Order groceries online and have them delivered to your door.

- **Google Maps:** Navigate anywhere, whether you're driving, walking, or taking public transit.

Overcoming Tech Hesitation

If the thought of learning new technology feels overwhelming, you're not alone. But like anything else, it gets easier with practice.

1. Start Small

Pick one tool to focus on, like texting or Zoom, and practice until it feels comfortable. Once you've mastered one, move on to the next.

2. Ask for Help

Your kids or grandkids are probably tech pros. Don't be afraid to ask them for guidance. Most of them will be thrilled to help.

3. Celebrate Your Wins

Every time you send a text, join a video call, or successfully avoid a scam, give yourself credit. Those small victories add up.

Action Steps for the Week

Here's your mission:

1. **Send a Text:** Pick one person and send them a quick "Hi, thinking of you!" message.

2. **Try a Video Call:** Schedule a Zoom or FaceTime call with a friend or family member.

3. **Set Up an App:** Download one app (like WhatsApp or Google Maps) and explore its features.

Conclusion: Building Your Bridge

Technology isn't just a tool, it's a bridge. It connects you to the people you care about, helps you stay informed, and can even make your daily life easier. You don't have to master it all at once. Start small, stay curious, and remember: every step you take is another plank on the bridge to a more connected, fulfilling life.

"Technology isn't just for the young, it's for the young at heart."

Thrive After 70: "The Veteran's Guide to Living Fully and Aging Gracefully"

Part 3:

Rediscovering Purpose & Joy

Chapter Seven

What's Next?

"Because the Best Chapters Are Still Ahead"

Let me tell you about a guy named Pete. Pete and I served together back in the day. Tough as nails, but with a heart big enough to carry the world. After the service, Pete did what so many of us did, he threw himself into work and family. He built a career, raised two kids, and wore that "provider" badge with pride. But here's the thing: by the time Pete hit 72, all of that was behind him. He was retired, the kids were busy with their own lives, and the quiet days started to stretch longer than he liked.

One day, Pete called me out of the blue. "Aaron," he said, "I feel like I'm just… waiting. And I don't know what I'm waiting for."

That hit me hard. Pete, the guy who once tackled life head-on, now felt like a ship drifting without a map. But here's the thing about Pete, he wasn't done yet. He just needed a reminder that life still had more to offer. So, we talked. I asked him, "What's something you've always wanted to do but never had the time for?" Pete thought about it, then laughed. "I always wanted to build furniture," he said. "Don't know if I'd be any good at it, but I've always loved the idea."

Long story short, Pete bought himself some tools, started small, and now spends his days in his garage workshop. But here's the best part: he doesn't just make furniture for himself. Pete started building benches for his local park and fixing up furniture for neighbors who couldn't afford new pieces. He's got purpose, community, and a whole lot of sawdust in his hair, and I've never seen him happier.

Why Finding Purpose Is So Important

Pete's story isn't unique. Maybe you've felt it too, that nagging question of *what now?* But here's the truth: life doesn't have to slow down just because you've hit a certain age. In fact, this can be one of the most exciting and meaningful chapters of your life.

Purpose isn't about big, flashy accomplishments. It's about waking up in the morning with something to look forward to, something that makes you feel alive and connected. Whether it's a new hobby, helping others, or learning something new, purpose is what gives life its spark.

Finding Purpose Through Volunteering and Mentorship

If you're not sure where to start, volunteering is one of the easiest ways to rediscover purpose. Giving your time and energy to help others doesn't just change their lives, it changes yours.

Pete's Bench Story Continued

Pete's first project, a simple park bench, turned into something bigger than he ever expected. When the park manager heard about it, he asked Pete if he'd be willing to mentor some teenagers in the community center's woodworking program. Pete hesitated at first, wondering what he could teach them. But after just one session, he was hooked. "Aaron," he told me, "those kids reminded me of my own grandkids, curious, a little lost, and just looking for someone to believe in them."

Ideas for Volunteering

You don't have to build furniture to make a difference. Here are a few ways you can start:

1. **Community Organizations**: Libraries, food banks, and senior centers are always looking for helping hands.

2. **Schools**: Offer to tutor, read to kids, or help with school events.

3. **Veterans' Groups**: If you're a veteran, your local VFW, American Legion, or VA can connect you with opportunities to mentor or advocate for others.

4. **Animal Shelters**: If you're an animal lover, shelters often need volunteers to walk dogs, clean kennels, or help with adoptions.

Discovering New Skills or Interests

Sometimes, finding purpose is about trying something completely new, something you've never had the time, courage, or opportunity to explore before.

Uncle Aaron's "Disaster Painting" Story

When I turned 52, I had to take an art course as part of my degree studies. Now, I didn't pick it because I thought I'd be good at it, I picked it because it sounded like a way to shake things up and try something completely out of my comfort zone. Let me tell you, my first painting looked like I'd let a toddler loose with finger paints. I think the professor was being generous when she called it "abstract."

But here's the thing: it was fun. There was something about the act of creating, just letting the brush move across the canvas, that felt freeing. I wasn't worried about being perfect or even being good. I was just doing it for the experience.

And after a few tries (and a lot of tips from classmates who were way better than me), I started to get the hang of it. My work wasn't going to hang in any galleries, but I didn't care. It became my way to unwind, to explore a part of myself I didn't even know was there. These days, I still paint from time to time. I've even gifted a few paintings to friends, though I always tell them, "Don't hang this where people will see it!"

The point is it wasn't about the end result. It was about the process, the joy of trying something new, and the surprise of finding a little spark where I didn't expect it.

Where to Start

Here are some ideas for discovering new skills or interests:

1. Take a Class

Whether online or in person, taking a class is a great way to learn something new while connecting with others who share your curiosity. Local libraries, senior centers, and community colleges often offer affordable or free courses. You could try painting (just like me!), cooking, photography, or even ballroom dancing. The goal isn't to master it, it's to enjoy the process.

Join a Club or Group

Shared interests are a great foundation for friendships. Love to read? Join a book club. Curious about gardening? Find a local group where you can trade tips and seedlings. If you're more into storytelling, check out a writers' circle or genealogy club. These groups are often full of welcoming people who love to share their passions.

Experiment at Home

The internet makes learning at home easier than ever. Want to try yoga? There's a YouTube channel for that. Curious about baking bread? There's an online tutorial for that too. The beauty of experimenting at home is that it's low pressure, you can try things at your own pace, without an audience.

Dive Into Technology

If you've been hesitant to try out technology, this might be the perfect time to dive in. Apps and platforms like YouTube, Duolingo, or even virtual reality can open up a world of new experiences. Technology doesn't have to feel overwhelming, it's just another tool for discovering what excites you.

Getting Involved in Community Initiatives

For many people, purpose comes from connecting with their community. It's about making a difference, building relationships, and feeling like you're part of something bigger.

1. Local Opportunities Abound

Your community is full of opportunities to get involved. You just need to know where to look.

- **Community Boards:** Check the bulletin boards at your local library, grocery store, or church for notices about events or volunteer opportunities.

- **Senior Centers:** These often host events, classes, and initiatives specifically for older adults.

- **Facebook Groups or Nextdoor:** Social media platforms have local groups where you can find out what's happening in your area.

2. Join or Start a Group Initiative

If there's a cause or project you care about, chances are there's already a group dedicated to it. From neighborhood clean-ups to food pantry drives, joining an initiative can help you meet like-minded people while giving back.

If you don't see a group for what you're passionate about, start one! It could be as simple as organizing a weekly walking group in your neighborhood or setting up a book exchange box in your local park.

3. Tap Into Your Unique Skills

Think about the skills or talents you've developed over the years. Maybe you're a great organizer, a skilled craftsman, or an excellent listener. Those skills are valuable to your community. Offer them up!

For example:

- Are you a former teacher? Offer tutoring or mentoring to local kids.

- Love to cook? Host a community potluck or teach a cooking class.

- Skilled at fixing things? Volunteer to help neighbors with small repairs or maintenance tasks.

Overcoming Obstacles to Finding Purpose

It's easy to get excited about the idea of rediscovering purpose, but let's address the obstacles that might be holding you back. Whether it's a lack of confidence, health challenges, or simply not knowing where to start, there's always a way forward.

1. "I'm Too Old to Start Something New"

I hear this all the time, and let me tell you, it's just not true. Learning and growth have no expiration date. Think of all the people who reinvented themselves later in life: Grandma Moses didn't start painting until she was in her 70s, and she became one of the most celebrated artists of her time. If they can do it, so can you.

2. "I Don't Know Where to Begin"

Sometimes, the hardest part is taking that first step. Here's a tip: don't overthink it. Start small. Pick one thing that sounds interesting and give it a try. It doesn't have to be perfect; it just has to be something.

3. "I Have Health Limitations"

If mobility or other health issues make certain activities difficult, look for alternatives.

- **Volunteer from Home:** Many organizations need help with phone calls, emails, or administrative tasks.

- **Virtual Classes:** Explore online learning platforms that let you participate without leaving home.

- **Adapted Hobbies:** Choose hobbies that match your physical abilities, like birdwatching, knitting, or storytelling.

Action Steps for the Week

Here's your purpose-finding mission:

1. **Write It Down:** Spend 10 minutes reflecting on what excites or inspires you. Write down three things you've always wanted to try.

2. **Take One Step:** Choose one of those ideas and commit to exploring it this week, whether that's signing up for a class, making a call, or gathering supplies.

3. **Get Involved:** Find one local event, group, or initiative to participate in this month.

Conclusion: The Best is Yet to Come

Here's the thing about purpose, it's not something you find once and keep forever. It changes as you change, evolves as you evolve. What matters is staying open to new experiences and giving yourself permission to explore. This stage of life isn't about winding down, it's about expanding, rediscovering, and creating something meaningful.

If Pete could find his purpose in a garage full of sawdust and teenagers, and I could find mine with a paintbrush and a shaky easel, I know you can find yours too.

"The next chapter of your life is waiting, and it's going to be a good one."

Chapter 8:

The Power of Storytelling

"Because Your Story Deserves to Be Told"

Let me tell you about Bobby G. He was a Vietnam veteran, serving in '64 and '65, and a father to one of my closest friends. But more than that, he was a childhood friend of my father's, the kind of guy you couldn't miss, even if you wanted to. He stood all of 5'6" but somehow managed to fill every room he walked into. Bobby G was one of those rare people who commanded respect just by being himself.

He was a former Marine with a bark as sharp as his bite, and trust me, neither one was for show. But beneath that tough exterior was someone who cared deeply about his community, about history, and about the lessons he could pass down to the next generation. He coached my softball teams when I was a kid and taught me how to march at 11 years old in the Boys and Girls Club. And he didn't just teach me how to put one foot in front of the other, he taught me how to walk with purpose.

Bobby G loved to tell stories. And as I sat with him and the other veterans at Post 8, I realized those stories were more than just entertainment, they were threads in the fabric of history, the history I desperately wanted to be a part of. I didn't fully grasp it then, but those stories planted seeds that would grow into the values, lessons, and perspectives I carry with me today.

Now, here I am, 40 years later, sharing Bobby G's stories, and the stories of so many others, with anyone who'll listen. That's the power of storytelling. It's not just about keeping memories alive; it's about carrying forward the lessons and wisdom that shaped who we are.

Why Your Story Matters

Whether you realize it or not, your story is part of something bigger. It's a piece of the puzzle that connects you to your family, your community, and even history itself. You might think your life is just "ordinary," but trust me, there's someone out there who can learn from your experiences, who can laugh at your anecdotes, or who can find comfort in knowing they're not alone.

1. Stories Connect Us

When you share your story, you build bridges between generations. Your children and grandchildren get to see the world through your eyes and understand the events, challenges, and triumphs that shaped your life.

2. Stories Preserve History

History isn't just what's written in textbooks. It's the lived experiences of people like Bobby G, like you, like me. By telling your story, you contribute to a collective history that might otherwise be forgotten.

3. Stories Teach Lessons

Every story holds a lesson, whether it's about perseverance, love, loss, or resilience. The wisdom you've gained through your life is a gift, and sharing it is one of the most powerful ways to leave a legacy.

Capturing Your Life Stories

So, how do you start telling your story? The good news is, you don't need to write a novel or have a perfect memory. All you need is the desire to share.

1. Start with One Memory

Think of one moment in your life that made you laugh, cry, or feel proud. Maybe it was the first time you held your child, the day you graduated boot camp, or even a funny moment you shared with a friend.

Example from Bobby G:

Bobby G used to tell a story about his first day in Vietnam. He said, "I thought I was ready for anything. Then I stepped off the plane, and the heat hit me like a wall. I looked around at the other guys, and we all had the same thought: *What the hell did we just get ourselves into?*" That memory wasn't just about the heat, it was about humility, about realizing that no matter how prepared you think you are, life has a way of surprising you.

2. Focus on Themes

If you're struggling to start, focus on specific themes:

- **Childhood Adventures:** What games did you play? Who were your closest friends?

- **Military Service or Work Life:** What was your proudest moment? What lessons did you learn?

- **Family and Relationships:** Who influenced you the most, and how?

Storytelling Exercises to Get You Started

If putting pen to paper feels daunting, these exercises can help you get the words flowing:

1. The "Firsts" Exercise

Make a list of "firsts" in your life, first job, first car, first big mistake. Pick one and write down everything you remember about it.

2. The Hero's Journey

Write about a time when you faced a challenge and overcame it. What did you learn about yourself?

3. The Time Capsule Prompt

Imagine you're creating a time capsule for your family to open 50 years from now. What would you want them to know about your life?

4. The Best Advice You Ever Got

Write down the best piece of advice someone ever gave you, and the story behind it.

Preserving and Sharing Your Story

Once you've started capturing your stories, think about how you want to preserve and share them.

1. Analog Options

- **Journals:** A simple notebook can be your best friend. Write in it regularly and let your thoughts flow freely.

- **Scrapbooks:** Combine photos, memorabilia, and written memories to create a keepsake for your family.

2. Digital Tools

- **Voice Recordings:** Use your phone to record yourself telling stories. Apps like Voice Memos (iPhone) or Easy Voice Recorder (Android) make it simple.

- **StoryCorps App:** This free app guides you through creating a recorded interview or story to share with family or even contribute to the Library of Congress.

3. Collaborative Projects

Involve your family in the storytelling process. Create a family tree, interview relatives, or start a shared document where everyone can contribute their memories.

Overcoming Common Storytelling Challenges

Let's tackle the most common reasons people hesitate to share their stories, and why you shouldn't let them hold you back.

1. "My Life Isn't Interesting"

Bobby G would have laughed at this one. He used to say, "Every life is interesting if you pay attention." Your story doesn't have to be dramatic to be meaningful. Sometimes, it's the small, everyday moments that resonate the most.

2. "I Don't Know Where to Start"

Start small. Pick one memory, one moment, or one lesson. Don't worry about structure or flow, just get it out.

3. "I'm Not a Writer"

Good news! you don't need to be. Your story doesn't have to be polished or perfect. The heart of it is what matters.

Action Steps for the Week

Here's your storytelling mission:

1. **Choose One Memory:** Spend 10 minutes writing or recording a story from your life.

2. **Share It:** Call a family member or friend and tell them the story.

3. **Document It:** Use a journal, voice recorder, or digital tool to preserve the story for future generations.

Conclusion: Your Story Is Your Legacy

Bobby G's stories didn't just entertain me, they shaped me. They reminded me of where I come from, what matters most, and the kind of person I want to be. Your stories can do the same for your family, your friends, and even people you've never met.

You've lived a life worth remembering. Now it's time to make sure your stories live on, too.

"Your story is your legacy. Share it, and it will never be forgotten."

Chapter 9:

Living Fully, Aging Gracefully

"Because It's Never Too Late to Make Everyday Count"

Let me tell you about Gladys. She was 78 when I met her. A WWII Women's Army Corps (WAC) veteran, Gladys was the kind of person who made an impression the moment you met her. We were filming for a local female veterans' organization a few years ago, and she had this energy that drew people in, calm but confident, quiet but full of purpose.

We got to talking, and she told me about her life, her years of service, the challenges she faced after the war, and the adventures she refused to let slip by. She wasn't loud about it, but Gladys had done things that most people would never dream of.

She was 78 when she went skydiving for the first time. "Why not?" she told me, shrugging like it was no big deal. "I figured if I could jump into life at 18 and serve during a war, I could jump out of a plane at 78." She had a twinkle in her eye that said she was just getting started. And she was. After that, Gladys picked up painting, joined a gardening club, and traveled to Yellowstone, a place she'd dreamed of seeing since she was a kid.

Talking to Gladys changed the way I think about aging. She wasn't waiting for life to happen, she was out there chasing it, creating it, and savoring every moment. She didn't let her age define her. Instead, she used it as motivation to embrace every opportunity she could.

Why Living Fully Matters

Gladys taught me something important: living fully isn't about being fearless or carefree. It's about being intentional with your time, staying curious, and finding joy in both the big adventures and the small, quiet moments.

Here's why it's so important:

1. **It Keeps You Engaged**: Trying new things and pursuing your passions stimulates your mind, challenges your perspective, and keeps life exciting.

2. **It Boosts Your Mood**: Studies show that stepping outside your comfort zone and engaging in new experiences releases dopamine, the "feel-good" chemical in your brain.

3. **It Strengthens Relationships**: Shared experiences, whether it's a trip, a hobby, or even a weekly coffee date, deepen your connections with others.

Creating Your Bucket List

Gladys had a bucket list, and she made sure to cross things off, one jump and one painting at a time. You can do the same. A bucket list isn't about grand, expensive adventures, it's about identifying what excites, inspires, or challenges you and finding ways to make it happen.

1. Start Small

Your bucket list doesn't need to start with something big like skydiving. Sometimes, the most meaningful goals are the simplest:

- Visiting a park you've never been to.

- Trying a recipe you've always been curious about.

- Writing a letter to someone you haven't spoken to in years.

2. Think Big

At the same time, don't be afraid to dream. Maybe you've always wanted to learn to play the guitar, visit Italy, or hike a scenic trail. Big goals give you something to work toward and look forward to.

3. Mix It Up

Include a variety of goals, some that are quick wins, and some that might take a little more time and effort. For example:

- **Quick Wins:** Try sushi for the first time, host a family dinner, or plant a flower garden.

- **Longer-Term Goals:** Take a road trip, learn a new skill, or volunteer regularly.

Example from Uncle Aaron

"When I turned 50, I made a bucket list, and at the top of it was taking my son to see the Grand Canyon. We packed up the car, hit the road, and when we got there, we just stood on the edge, staring at something so much bigger than ourselves. It was humbling and awe-inspiring, and I'm so glad I made it happen."

Exploring Travel Opportunities and Fun Activities on a Budget

Travel and new experiences don't have to cost a fortune. There are plenty of ways to explore, enjoy, and create memories without draining your savings.

1. Local Adventures

You don't have to go far to find something new. Start with what's right in your own backyard:

- Visit local museums, parks, or historical sites.

- Try a new restaurant or café.

- Attend free events like concerts, farmers' markets, or community festivals.

2. Affordable Travel Tips

If you're dreaming of bigger adventures, here's how to make them happen on a budget:

- **Road Trips:** Gas is often cheaper than plane tickets, and the journey itself can be an adventure.

- **Off-Season Travel:** Visit popular destinations during their off-season for lower prices and fewer crowds.

- **Senior Discounts:** Many attractions and tours offer discounts specifically for older adults.

- **Travel Clubs:** Join organizations like Road Scholar, which offer affordable trips designed for lifelong learners.

3. Free Fun

Some of the best experiences don't cost a dime:

- Watch the sunrise or sunset.

- Explore a new walking trail.

- Host a potluck or game night with friends.

Staying Optimistic and Engaged Despite Challenges

Life isn't always smooth sailing, and challenges, whether physical, emotional, or financial, can make it harder to embrace new experiences. But here's what I've learned from people like Gladys: even when things are tough, there's always something to be grateful for, something to look forward to, and something you can do to make life a little brighter.

1. Focus on What You Can Do

If health or mobility is a challenge, adapt your goals to fit your abilities:

- If you love hiking but can't manage the trails anymore, try a paved nature walk or a visit to a botanical garden.

- If long trips aren't possible, explore virtual tours of museums or landmarks from the comfort of your home.

2. Practice Gratitude

Gratitude is one of the most powerful tools for staying optimistic. Take a few minutes each day to reflect on what you're thankful for, whether it's a sunny day, a kind word, or a favorite meal.

3. Surround Yourself with Positivity

The people you spend time with have a big impact on your mindset. Seek out friends or groups that inspire you, lift you up, and encourage you to keep growing.

Practical Tips for Living Fully

Here are a few simple ways to make everyday count:

1. **Say Yes More Often**: The next time someone invites you to do something, whether it's a walk, a lunch date, or a community event, resist the urge to say no.

2. **Stay Curious**: Read books, watch documentaries, or take classes to keep learning and exploring.

3. **Celebrate Small Wins**: Whether it's finishing a puzzle, baking a cake, or organizing your closet, find joy in the little victories.

Action Steps for the Week

Here's how to start living fully this week:

1. **Write Your Bucket List**: Take 10 minutes to write down 10 things you'd like to do, big or small.

2. **Plan One Activity**: Choose one item from your list and make a plan to do it this week.

3. **Invite Someone Along**: Share the experience with a friend or family member.

Conclusion: Every Day is a New Opportunity

When I think about Gladys, I don't just think about her skydiving story. I think about the way she approached life, with curiosity, courage, and gratitude. She didn't let her age, or anything else, hold her back.

You have that same opportunity. Whether it's trying something new, reconnecting with old passions, or simply savoring the moment, every day holds the potential for joy.

So, what's next for you? Whatever it is, I hope you approach it with the boldness of Gladys and the wonder of standing on the edge of the Grand Canyon for the first time.

"Life doesn't end at 70, it starts again, with a little more wisdom and a lot more freedom."

End Chapter:

Resources and Tools for Thriving After 70

This chapter is a guide to the research, tools, and trusted resources that inspired the strategies shared throughout this book. Whether you want to explore specific topics in greater depth, access helpful tools, or connect with trusted organizations, this section will point you in the right direction. The goal is to empower you with the confidence and knowledge to live fully and age gracefully.

Highlighted Research and Key Data

Social Security Strategies

Stat: Delaying Social Security benefits until age 70 increases payouts by approximately 8% per year beyond full retirement age.

- **Source:** Social Security Administration (SSA), www.ssa.gov

Exercise for Healthy Aging

Stat: Regular low-impact exercise, such as walking or tai chi, reduces joint stiffness and improves mobility by increasing synovial fluid production.

- **Source:** Harvard Medical School, "The Health Benefits of Walking" (2021).

Benefits of Social Connection

Stat: Older adults with strong social networks have a 50% greater likelihood of living longer than those who are socially isolated.

- **Source:** National Institute on Aging (NIA), "Social Isolation and Loneliness in Older Adults" (2020).

Mental Health and Mindfulness

Stat: Mindfulness-Based Stress Reduction (MBSR) programs reduce chronic pain intensity and improve quality of life by 43% in older adults.

- **Source:** National Institutes of Health (NIH), Research on Mindfulness and Aging (2019).

Practical Resources for Financial Security

Social Security and Benefits Management

- **My Social Security:** Create an account to access your earnings record, manage benefits, and estimate future payouts. www.ssa.gov/myaccount

- **Veterans Benefits:** Explore and apply for VA benefits, including disability compensation and pension programs. www.va.gov

Budgeting and Financial Tools

- **Mint:** A free app for tracking expenses, creating budgets, and managing financial goals. www.mint.com

- **Personal Capital:** A financial planning tool that helps retirees manage savings, investments, and withdrawal strategies.
www.personalcapital.com

Estate Planning Resources

- **LegalZoom:** Provides affordable solutions for creating wills, trusts, and other essential legal documents.
www.legalzoom.com

- **Everplans:** A digital platform to organize and store important documents, including medical directives, wills, and passwords.
www.everplans.com

Health and Wellness Resources

Exercise Programs for Older Adults

- **SilverSneakers:** Offers free or discounted fitness classes and gym access for seniors. Check eligibility through your Medicare Advantage plan.
www.silversneakers.com

- **National Senior Games Association (NSGA):** A community for older adults to participate in competitive and recreational sports.
www.nsga.com

Mental Health and Stress Management

- **Headspace for Seniors:** A mindfulness and meditation app tailored for older adults, with guided sessions to reduce stress and improve focus.
www.headspace.com

- **Veterans Crisis Line:** Support for veterans experiencing mental health challenges or crises.
Dial 988, then press 1 or visit www.veteranscrisisline.net

Social Connection and Purpose

Building Community

- **Meetup:** Find local groups and events based on your interests, from hiking clubs to book groups.
  www.meetup.com

- **VolunteerMatch:** Discover volunteer opportunities in your area, tailored to your interests and schedule.
  www.volunteermatch.org

Purpose and Mentorship

- **Encore.org:** Connects older adults with opportunities to mentor or work on purpose-driven projects.
  www.encore.org

- **Big Brothers Big Sisters:** An organization that matches seniors with young people who can benefit from mentorship.
  www.bbbs.org

Tools for Action

Daily Activity and Health Logs

- **Exercise Tracker:** Use a notebook or app to track daily movement, stretching, or fitness routines. For example, log steps, resistance training, or time spent walking.

Financial Planning Checklist

- List your income sources (Social Security, VA benefits, pensions).

- Map out your monthly expenses.

- Set withdrawal strategies for retirement accounts.

Legacy Binder Checklist

- Include essential documents:

    - Will and medical directives.

- Financial account information.
- Personal letters for family or loved ones.

FAQs and Common Questions

What are Required Minimum Distributions (RMDs)?

RMDs are withdrawals the IRS requires from certain retirement accounts (e.g., 401(k), traditional IRA) starting at age 73. Failure to withdraw the minimum amount may result in penalties.

How do I apply for VA Aid and Attendance benefits?

Visit www.va.gov or contact a Veterans Service Officer (VSO) to assist with the application process.

What's the best way to find low-impact exercise programs?

Check with local gyms, senior centers, or Medicare Advantage plans to see if they offer access to programs like SilverSneakers or aquatic classes.

Closing Thoughts

This chapter is a resource to help you take action, connect with trusted organizations, and feel confident in planning the years ahead. Remember, thriving after 70 is about using the right tools, finding support, and embracing the opportunities available to you. Take it one step at a time and always know there are resources and people ready to help you succeed.

Thrive After 70: "The Veteran's Guide to Living Fully and Aging Gracefully"

The Next Chapter of Your Journey

"Because Every Chapter of Life Deserves to Be Lived Fully"

Let me leave you with this: your story is far from over. If you've made it this far through *"Thrive After 70: The Veteran's Guide to Living Fully and Aging Gracefully,"* you already know this isn't about slowing down. It's about embracing the life you've built, finding new joys, and creating a legacy that reflects the values and love you've shared along the way.

You've read stories about people like Gladys, Bobby G, and Pete, individuals who didn't let age define them. Instead, they lived with purpose, curiosity, and a sense of adventure. But here's the thing: *your* story has just as much power. Whether you've already started crossing things off your bucket list or are still figuring out what brings you joy, this is your time to thrive.

But living fully is just one part of the journey. The next step is about ensuring that what you've worked so hard to build is protected. It's about making sure the people you love are taken care of and that your legacy reflects the life you've lived.

What Comes Next: Building Your Legacy

The next book in this series, *"Legacy Secured: Protect Your Finances, Family, and Future,"* will guide you through everything you need to know to protect your loved ones, your assets, and your peace of mind. We'll break down the topics that can feel overwhelming, like retirement planning, insurance, estate preparation, and handling the unexpected, into simple, actionable steps.

Here's a preview of what's inside:

- **Managing Your Retirement Income:** Learn how to make your money work for you and avoid common financial pitfalls.

- **Protecting Your Assets:** From understanding trusts to managing property insurance, we'll cover the strategies that safeguard what matters most.

- **Creating a Legacy Plan:** Whether it's setting up a will, choosing beneficiaries, or supporting causes you care about, this book will help you leave a lasting impact.

- **Preparing for the Unexpected:** We'll discuss how to navigate healthcare costs, long-term care, and emergency planning with confidence.

But this isn't just a financial guide. It's about creating a future where you, and the people you love, feel secure, supported, and prepared.

More Resources to Support Your Journey

In addition to *"Legacy Secured,"* I've written other books that may help you or the people you care about navigate life's challenges. Here's how they might bring value to your journey:

- **For Your Grandkids or Younger Family Members:**
"The SEL Leadership Playbook" and *"Master Mindset"* are packed with tools for building emotional intelligence, resilience, and leadership skills. If you've got teenagers or young adults in your life who could use a boost in navigating today's fast-paced world, these books are a great place to start.

- **For Aspiring Entrepreneurs or Go-Getters in Your Family:**
"The Entrepreneur's Playbook: Strategies for Success" and *"The Leadership Playbook"* are all about helping people build confidence, take smart risks, and grow into leaders in their careers or businesses.

- **For Anyone Who Wants to Build Financial Freedom:**
"Budget Like a Boss: Uncle Aaron's Straight-Talk Guide to Mastering Your Money" is a no-nonsense guide to getting your

finances in order, whether you're starting fresh or trying to reach the next level of financial independence.

- **For Veterans and Their Families:**
  If you're part of the veteran community, or have loved ones who are, my upcoming book *"Thrive After 70: The Veteran's Guide to Living Fully and Aging Gracefully"* and *"Legacy Secured"* are must-reads. Together, they provide the tools you need to navigate aging, finances, and leaving a meaningful legacy.

Whether it's for you or someone in your circle, these books are here to empower, educate, and inspire.

Your Next Step: Reflect and Prepare

As you close this book, I want you to take a moment to reflect on these questions:

1. What are the experiences and moments that bring you the most joy?

2. How do you want to be remembered by the people you love?

3. Have you taken steps to ensure your legacy reflects your values and protects your family?

The answers to these questions will guide you as we move into *"Legacy Secured."* This next chapter isn't just about finances, it's about making thoughtful choices today that protect the people you care about and leave them with a sense of love, security, and gratitude for all you've done.

Every Chapter is an Opportunity

If there's one thing I hope you take away from this book, it's that life after 70 isn't about "winding down." It's about living with purpose, savoring every moment, and creating a future you're proud of. The stories you tell, the experiences you embrace, and the legacy you leave will carry your spirit forward for generations.

You've already proven that you have the strength, resilience, and wisdom to face life's challenges head-on. Now, let's make sure that legacy lives on.

So, go ahead: try something new, reconnect with old friends, share your stories, and embrace the life that's still unfolding in front of you. And when you're ready, turn the page and join me in *"Legacy Secured."* Together, we'll navigate the next part of this journey with clarity, confidence, and a whole lot of heart.

"You've lived a life worth celebrating. Now, let's make sure your story, your family, and your legacy are protected for the future."

– Uncle Aaron

Thrive After 70: "The Veteran's Guide to Living Fully and Aging Gracefully"

www.ingramcontent.com/pod-product-compliance
Lightning Source LLC
Chambersburg PA
CBHW061338140726
47997CB00003B/1012